ΤΣΟΥΚΑΛΑ

Ο ΚΑΠΕΤΑΝ ΒΡΥΚΟΛΑΚΑΣ

ΕΚΔΟΤΙΚΟΝ ΚΑΤΑΣΤΗΜΑ
ΑΛ. & ΕΥΑΓ. ΠΑΠΑΔΗΜΗΤΡΙΟΥ
ΣΟΦΟΚΛΕΟΥΣ 53 - ΑΘΗΝΑΙ

Greek Vampires

George Horton

NOTE ON THE TEXT

In 1929, the U.S. diplomat, writer and philhellenist George Horton (1859-1942) published a book with the rather curious title "Home of Nymphs and Vampires: The Isles of Greece."

As alluring as the title may seem, only a few chapters in Horton's book focused specifically on the folklore of vampires and fairies throughout the islands of Greece.

The eighth chapter of the book, simply titled "Vampires", remains a gripping account of the history and legends surrounding Greek vampires, commonly known as the *vrykolakas*.

With the original book being long out-of-print, and with no digitised copy available online, Horton's small text serves as a perfect introduction to Greek vampirology for the anglophone reader, and thus merits its own volume.

The appendix to Horton's text includes an early eyewitness account of the superstitions surrounding the *vrykolakas* on the island of Mykonos in 1700.

GREEK VAMPIRES

Home of Nymphs
and Vampires

George Horton

Home of Nymphs and Vampires: The Isles of Greece
by George Horton

GREEK VAMPIRES

The island of Santorini became notorious in the seventeenth century as a nest of vampires, and this evil reputation clung to it for many generations. Even today one hears the expression, "to send vampires to Santorini," which is equivalent to "sending coals to Newcastle" or "owls to Athens," the more classical comparison.

Exactly what is a vampire? The conception, as it exists in the mind of the uneducated and superstitious Greek peasant, varies somewhat. There are vampires that associate with human beings, perform the duties and engage in the callings of ordinary people, and even intermarry with them and procreate children. There are others that are fearful and malignant demons, wreaking destruction on all who come within their way. Perhaps we might make a broad classification of harmless and evil vampires, though both kinds are unpopular. The harmless species seems to be an ancient and more purely Hellenic conception, the malignant, a Slavic grafting; this latter being the most dreadful and revolting superstition that has ever obsessed the human mind.

In the Middle Ages vampirism was officially recognized by the Church, and implicitly believed in. Writers of the highest standing discussed it seriously and testified to its existence as eyewitnesses. A vampire, or *vrykolakas* in modern Greek, was supposed to be a human body that had lain in the ground without decomposing, and that rose from the grave and prowled about, bent on mischief. The devil, or one of his imps, entered the carcass, taking the place of the evacuated soul. I cannot imagine a more terrifying or revolting conception.

As bodies were believed to lie longer in the dry volcanic dust of Santorini than elsewhere without decomposing, that island became celebrated as peculiarly adapted to the production of these dreadful beings. Prayers and ceremonies were prescribed by the Church for the laying of vampires; but the most radical cure was the disinterring and burning by the villagers of the suspected corpse, and this was frequently done, to an accompaniment of prayers chanted by the priest. The spread of popular education and legislation have done much toward the suppression of this superstition and the gruesome practises resulting from it, but it still lingers on to a certain extent, and I myself have come across it.

The vampire, as it existed in the popular imagination of the seventeenth century, is thus described by Leo Allatius, a writer of that epoch:

> The *vrykolakas* is the body of a man of evil and immoral life—very often of one who has been excommunicated by his bishop. Such bodies do not, like those of other dead men, suffer decomposition after burial nor turn to dust, but having, as it appears, a skin of extreme toughness, become swollen and extended all over, so that the joints can scarcely be bent; the skin becomes stretched like the parchment of a drum, and when struck gives out the same sound.
>
> Into such a body the devil enters, and, issuing from the tomb, goes about, chiefly at night, knocking at doors and calling one of the household. If such one answers, he dies the next day; but a *vrykolakas* never calls twice, and so the inhabitants of the isle of Chios never answer at night a first knocking at their doors.

This monster is said to be so destructive to men that, appearing actually in the daytime, even at noon—and that not only in houses but in fields and highroads and enclosed vineyards—by its mere aspect and without either speech or touch kills them.

This is not difficult to believe. Many people would die of fright on meeting such a monster.

Father François Richard, a Jesuit priest of the island of Santorini, confirmed in a written treatise the statements of Allatius, and added:

The devil works by means of dead bodies as well as by living sorcerers. These bodies he animates and preserves for a long time in their entirety; he appears with the face of the dead, traversing now the streets, and again the open country; he enters men's houses, leaving some horror stricken, others deprived of speech, and still others lifeless; here he inflicts violence, there loss and everywhere terror.

The vampires of which I have been told personally by servants and peasants during my long residence in Greece have possessed certain qualities not cited by the ancient writers, so far as I know; they have been described to me as possessing supernatural strength, and the power of flying through the air, and even of taking men along with them.

YANNI AND THE VAMPIRE

A villager by the name of Yanni went to sleep on the ground at the end of a hard day's work and did not awaken until night had fallen. He was aroused by hearing a voice, proceeding from the earth beneath him, calling, "Let me out! Let me out!"

Much wondering, he sprang to his feet, when a *vrykolakas* issued from the ground and stood beside him. It seems that he had been lying on his back above a grave with his arms stretched out, thus forming a cross, which sacred sign the vampire had been unable to pass.

This creature seized the villager by the hand and flew with him for a great distance through the air, till the two came to a palace on a hill. In through an open window they went, into the bed chamber of a beautiful maiden, fast asleep, with the moonlight streaming over her lovely face and long blonde hair scattered upon her pillow.

The *vrykolakas* killed and commenced to devour her, offering pieces of flesh to his terrified companion, with the words: "Eat, Yanni, eat, it's as sweet as Syros *loukoum!*"

The villager passed an exciting and extremely unpleasant night, but was greatly relieved when, just before daybreak, his grisly guide announced that he must return to his grave. The twain went sailing back through the air and in no time arrived at their starting place, where the vampire disappeared into the ground.

Yanni marked the place and brought a priest; as soon as he could find one. Appropriate prayers were read, which were so effective that the body disintegrated immediately. The peasants standing by could hear bones rattling on the coffin's bottom, so sudden was the dissolution. So ended that vampire.

This tale was told to me with much solemnity and many signings of the cross by a woman who had no doubt as to its veracity.

THE STORY OF PHILINNION

It is my own conviction that the conception of a dead body, preserved entire and tenanted by a devil, is not today the general Greek idea of a vampire, and certainly the Church has ceased to encourage this superstition.

The *vrykolakas* of today in Greece is a corpse

from which the spirit has not fled; a wretched being that is neither dead nor alive; that has the power to rise and circulate among the living, but that must return to the grave to sleep. It is the duty of all good Christians to see to it that a spirit so imprisoned is set free, either by prayers, or by the actual destruction of the body.

The general belief among the Orthodox, pervading even the better-educated classes, that the rapid dissolution of the mortal remains after death is a good omen, is an echo of the vampire superstition. The modern *vrykolakas* is usually of an evil, frequently malignant nature, but he is sometimes kindly and even benevolent. That the obsession in this form is purely Hellenic and ancient in origin is proved by the story of Philinnion, daughter of Demostratus and his wife Charito, who lived in the times of Hadrian.

Philinnion had been dead and her body laid away in the family vault for six months, when she was seen one night in her father's house by her old nurse. She had come to visit surreptitiously one Machates, a young man who was a guest of her parents.

The nurse ran to tell the mother, who promptly became hysterical and fainted away. Persuaded at last by the servant, she went and peeped into the room, where she indeed saw a girl that resembled her daughter. She determined to wait until morning before confronting her, but in the morning the girl was gone.

Machates was now questioned, who affirmed that he was not aware that Demostratus and Charito had lost a daughter by the name of Philinnion, but he exhibited a gold ring which the girl had given him and her breast band, which she had left behind. These were instantly recognized as belonging to Philinnion.

That night, therefore, the family kept watch, and, when Philinnion came, they entered the chamber. An affecting scene followed, at the end of which the fair but gruesome visitor dropped lifeless to the floor. There was great excitement in the town and a public meeting was held, at which it was decided that the family vault must be opened. This was done, and the shelf upon which the corpse of Philinnion had been laid was found vacant; only a ring and a gilt cup were there, presents which Machates had given her on one of her visits to him. Another public meeting was held, at which Hyllus, the town seer, advised that the body be burned and that certain religious ceremonies be performed, which counsels were acted upon. Machates committed suicide.

Now this is an ancient story which is modern

in all its details, even to the burning of the body and the participation of the priests.

THE VAMPIRE WHO EMIGRATED

It is not often that vampire stories contain a romantic element. The wanderings and adventures of a certain nameless vampire, of comparatively recent date, however, make a pretty good short story.

One of the nine recognized ways for producing a *vrykolakas* is for a cat to jump over the body before it is buried; and that is exactly what happened in the present case. Three days after the burial the sexton went to the cemetery at night and saw the dead man wandering around in his shroud. The good man fled in terror and spread the news. The next morning the islanders flocked to the grave, which they opened and found occupied. A great discussion arose, some maintaining that the sexton had been the victim of an illusion; others that he must certainly be in the right, as it was common knowledge that a cat had jumped over the corpse.

The next night the sexton returned to the cemetery with a number of friends, and they all plainly saw the spectre walking among the tombs. Numbers, it seems, did not give courage, for they all fled in terror.

The tomb was again reopened and found occupied. This happened three times in succession, when the priest was summoned and many prayers read over the grave, without effect. The *vrykolakas* even took courage, for he began to circulate about the village at night, rattling chains, knocking on windows, shouting, and generally making a nuisance of himself.

Suddenly all this ceased, and from that time on, quiet reigned on the island. The grave was again opened and found empty. The *vrykolakas* had gone to a village on a distant island, where he opened a general store and ultimately became rich. He even married a wife, but nobody knew what his name was, nor whence he came; they found his shop one morning open, with him in it, ready for business. The owner of the building said that his strange tenant had arrived one evening, rented the place, stocked it and was ready for customers in the morning.

The wife that he took—they gave him a wife because he had become rich and seemed a good man—gave birth to two children without bones. He never ate meat, but only the insides of slaughtered animals; and every Friday evening he went on a journey, from which he returned Sunday morning. No one knew where he went.

When his wife asked him, "Why do you never eat meat?" he replied: "In order to separate things inside from things outside."

When she inquired, "Why do you travel every Friday?" he answered: "Because then it is necessary to fill my house."

When she demanded of him, "Why are our children without bones?" he explained: "In order to separate those who are from those who are not."

But from these words she understood nothing at all.

After some time it chanced that the brother of the dead man travelled to that town; and as soon as the *vrykolakas* saw the brother he embraced and kissed him. The brother was frightened, but that one quieted him and took him to his house and kept and entertained him a long time. The brother saw everything: the abstinence from meat, the boneless children, the journeys every Friday. He learned much also from the wife, and became convinced that the merchant was a *vrykolakas*.

He determined, therefore, to leave immediately and return to his own country. The *vryko-*

lakas gave him much money and enjoined upon him to say nothing of the things that he had seen.

When the brother arrived in his native village, however, he told the whole story. The villagers went to the cemetery on Wednesday and opened the grave which they found empty. On Friday night they opened it again, and he was there. They tried to burn him, but he jumped up and started to run away. They had, however, taken the precaution to surround the place with a ring of burning sulphur, and stood waving torches, so that he could not escape. He cried, shouted, begged, but in vain. Then he prayed that he might be allowed to see his brother, if not all of him, then only so much as a finger.

So the brother was brought, covered up so that just one finger stuck out; and the *vrykolakas* jumped on him and swallowed him at one gulp. Then the fire burned him, the whole matter ended, and the village quieted down.

Now here we have a well-intentioned *vrykolakas*, of the classic type, who associates with the living and even takes a wife. He excites the reader's sympathy to such an extent that it is possible to appreciate the justice of the punishment inflicted on the faithless brother. He is capable of traversing long distances at electric speed, and of entering and issuing from his grave without disturbing the solid earth. In the original of this tale, which is told in the simple dialect of the islanders, the sepulchral hero is referred to as "This One," or "That One," and no name given to him.

THE SHOEMAKER VAMPIRE

From the island of Thera comes the well-known story of the shoemaker who died and became a *vrykolakas*. He appeared to his wife exactly as he had been in life. He mended the children's shoes, brought water from the cistern, and often was seen in the fields cutting wood for the house.

This went on for some time, until at last the people of the town were seized with fear. They therefore exhumed the body and burned it, after which he was seen no more.

THE VAMPIRE PLOWBOY

In Samos is told the story of a farmer's servant who so loved his master that after death he became a *vrykolakas* and continued to work for him. He went by night to the barn, yoked the oxen and ploughed while his master slept.

The neighbours wondered how the fields were ploughed so quickly, and they asked the farmer, who replied that he did not know. He himself worked all day and ploughed about three stremmas. (Stremma, one thousand square meters). When he went out in the morning he found six stremmas done, and his oxen covered with sweat and all tired out. He could not understand the thing at all and he feared the beasts would die of fatigue.

The neighbours suspected the truth and went and watched at night. They saw the servant come and yoke the oxen and set out for the field. So they opened the grave next day and burned the body, after which the wonder ceased.

How can one refuse to believe in *vrykolakes* (plural of *vrykolakas*) in the light of such testimony as this? One detail, at least, of these tales must be accepted as true: the measures taken by the villagers to rid themselves of these unwelcome "revenants."

One more story, also from the island of Thera, that nest of vampires, and I am through.

THE CLOTHES OF THE VRYKOLAKAS

Once upon a time there was a midwife, and she had a daughter. Moreover, in those times a rich man died. They buried him in a fine suit of clothes and a new hat, with his watch and his rings.

The midwife was sent for by a woman in childbirth and she said to her daughter, "Daughter, call in a neighbour to keep you company."

But the girl knew that they had buried the rich man in all his finery, and she said to herself: "I'll go open the grave and strip him, and afterward I'll call in the neighbour."

So she went, opened the grave, and took the clothes and everything of value. But she pulled so hard on one of the silk stockings that the foot came away with it, and she took it with her. She returned to the house and a neighbour woman came to spend the night with her. As they were sitting talking, there was a knocking at the door, as if someone wished to beat it down. A voice was heard: "Open and give me back my clothes and my foot."

This kept up all night. In the morning the neighbour ran to her house, nearly crazy with fear. The girl took the clothes and the foot and buried them. That night another neighbour woman, who knew nothing about the matter, came to stay with her, when again was heard the knocking and the voice: "Open and give me my clothes and my foot or I will drown you in the washtub."

The next evening nobody could be found who was willing to pass the night in the house, and the midwife had not yet returned. The girl was obliged to remain alone. The night was rainy and dark.

After some hours a voice was heard: "Open, my daughter. I am soaked here in the mud and the rain. Open quickly!"

The girl jumped up, crying, "O mama, I'm so glad you have come! I am all alone."

She opened the door and someone came in that she thought was her mother, who said: "Fill the washtub with water, as I wish to take a bath."

She obeyed, whereupon her visitor seized and dragged her to the tub, with the words: "I am the *vrykolakas*. Give me my foot and my clothes or I will hold your head under until you drown."

The girl replied, "They are not here, I have buried them."

He forced her to lead him through the stormy and dark night to the spot and dig up the foot and the clothes. Then he took her back to the house and drowned her. When the mother returned in the morning, she found her daughter dead.

. . .

For gruesomeness this tale leaves little to be desired, and has few rivals. One can only hope that the children of Santorini are not brought up on such stories.

The peculiar literary touch of all vampire stories is their weirdness. They are fantastic in the way the diseased brain of Poe produced gruesome effects. Yet we must not forget that *vrykolakes* were accepted as a matter of course by the leading churches not so long ago; and I am convinced that the superstition has by no means died out in Greece. This is especially true of the island villages and hamlets, which are practically untouched by the waves of change and progress that sweep over the rest of the world.

My attention was called quite recently to the case of a young man, an inhabitant of a seaside village near Smyrna, who rose at night and killed his bride of a few months because he had discovered, as he alleged, that she was a *vrykolakas*. The proofs that he brought forward were conclusive to him.

APPENDIX

VOYAGE

INTO THE

LEVANT:

Perform'd by Command of the Late *French* King.

CONTAINING

The Antient and Modern STATE of the Islands of the *Archipelago*; as also of *Constantinople*, the Coasts of the *Black Sea*, *Armenia*, *Georgia*, the Frontiers of *Persia*, and *Asia Minor*.

WITH

PLANS of the principal Towns and Places of Note; an Account of the Genius, Manners, Trade, and Religion of the respective People inhabiting those Parts: And an Explanation of Variety of Medals and Antique Monuments.

Illustrated with Full Descriptions and Curious Copper-Plates of great Numbers of Uncommon Plants, Animals, &c. And several Observations in Natural History.

By M. *TOURNEFORT*, of the Royal Academy of Sciences, Chief Botanist to the late *French* King, &c.

To which is Prefix'd,
The Author's LIFE, in a Letter to M. *Begon* : As also his Elogium, pronounc'd by M. *Fontenelle*, before a publick Assembly of the Academy of Sciences.

Adorn'd with an Accurate MAP of the Author's Travels, not in the *French* Edition : Done by Mr. *Senex*.

In TWO VOLUMES.

LONDON,

Printed for D. BROWNE, A. BELL, J. DARBY, A. BETTESWORTH, J. PEMBERTON, C. RIVINGTON, J. HOOKE, R. CRUTTENDEN and T. GUY, J. BATTLEY, E. SYMON. M.DCC.XVIII.

Title page from A Voyage Into the Levant *by Joseph Pitton de Tournefort, 1718, London*

The Exhumation of a Vampire on the Island of Mykonos in 1700

by Joseph Pitton de Tournefort

We were present at a very different scene, and one very barbarous, in the same island, which happened upon the occasion of one of those corpses, which they fancy to come to life again after their interment. The man whose story we are going to relate, was a peasant of Mykonos, naturally ill-natured and quarrelsome; this is a circumstance to be taken notice of in such cases: he was murdered in the fields, nobody knew how, or by whom. Two days after his being buried in a chapel in the town, it was noised about that he was seen to walk in the night with great haste, that he tumbled about peoples' goods, put out their lamps, grabbed them from behind, and a thousand other monkey tricks. At first the story was received with laughter; but the thing was looked upon to be serious, when the better sort of people began to complain of it; the *papas* (Orthodox priests) themselves gave credit to the fact, and no doubt had their reasons for so doing; the liturgy must be said, to be sure: but for all this, the peasant drove his old trade, and heeded nothing they could do. After divers meetings of the chief people of the city, of priests and monks, it was gravely concluded, that it was necessary, in consequence of some musty ceremonial, to wait till nine days after the interment.

On the tenth day they said one mass in the chapel where the body was laid, in order to drive out the demon which they imagined was got into it. After mass, they took the body and got everything ready for pulling out its heart. The butcher of the town, an old clumsy fellow, first opened the belly instead of the breast: he groped a long while among the entrails but could not find what he was looking for; at last, somebody told him he should cut up the diaphragm. The heart was pulled out, to the admiration of the spectators. In the meantime, the corpse stunk so abominably, that they were obliged to burn frankincense; but the smoke mixing with the exhalations from the carcass, increased the stink, and began to give the poor people a headache. Their imagination, struck with the spectacle before them, grew full of visions. It came into their noodles, that a thick smoke arose out of the body; we dare not say it was the smoke of the incense. They were incessantly bawling out "*vrykolakas!*" in the chapel and the place before it: this is the name they give to these pretended revenants. The noise bellowed through the streets, and it seemed to be a name invented on purpose to rend the roof of the chapel. Several there present averred that the wretch's blood was extremely red: the butcher swore the body was still warm; whence they concluded that the deceased was a very ill man for not being thoroughly dead, or in plain terms for suffering himself to be re-animated by *Old Nick*; which is the notion they have of a *vrykolakas*. They then roared out that name in a stupendous manner. Just at this time came in a flock of people, loudly protesting that they plainly perceived the body was not grown stiff, when it was carried from the fields to church to be buried, and that consequently it was a true *vrykolakas*; which word was still the burden of the song.

I don't doubt they would have sworn it did not stink, had not we been there; so amazed were the poor people with this disaster, and so infatuated with their notion of the dead being reanimated. As for us who were got as close to the corpse as we could, that we might be more exact in our observations, we were almost poisoned with the intolerable stink that issued from it. When they asked us what we thought of this body, we told them we believed it to be thoroughly dead: but as we were willing to cure, or at least not to exasperate their prejudiced imaginations, we represented to them, that it was no wonder the butcher should feel a little warmth when he groped among the entrails that were then rotting; that it was no extraordinary thing for it to emit fumes, since dung turned-up will do the same; that as for the pretended redness of the blood, it still appeared by the butcher's hands to be nothing but a very stinking nasty smear.

After all our reasons, they were of the opinion that it would be their wisest course to burn the dead man's heart on the seashore: but this execution did not make him a bit more tractable; he went on with his racket more furiously than ever: he was accused of beating folks in the night, breaking down doors, and even roofs of houses; clattering windows; tearing clothes; emptying bottles and vessels. It was the most thirsty devil! I believe he did not spare anybody but the consul in whose house we lodged. Nothing could be more miserable than the condition of this island; all the inhabitants seemed frightened out of their senses: the wisest among them were stricken like the rest: it was an epidemical disease of the brain, as dangerous and infectious as the madness of dogs. Whole families quitted their houses and brought their tent beds from the farthest parts of the town into the public place, there to spend the night. They were every instant complaining of some new insult; nothing was to be heard but sighs and groans at the approach of night: the better sort of people retired into the country.

When the prepossession was so general, we thought it our best way to hold our tongues. Had we opposed it, we had not only been accounted ridiculous blockheads, but atheists and infidels. How was it possible to stand against the madness of a whole people? Those that believed we doubted the truth of the fact came and upbraided us with our incredulity, and strove to prove that there was such a thing as the *vrykolakas,* by citing the *Buckler of Faith*, written by F. Richard, a Jesuit missionary. He was a *latin*, they say, and consequently you ought to give him credit. We should have got nothing by denying the justness of the consequence: it was as good as a comedy to us every morning, to hear the new follies committed by this night-bird; they charged him with being guilty of the most abominable sins.

Some citizens, that were most zealous for the good of the public, fancied that they had been deficient in the most material part of the ceremony. They were of the opinion that they had been wrong in saying mass before they had pulled out the wretch's heart: had we taken this precaution, they say, we'd have beat the devil, as sure as a gun; he would have hanged before he would ever have come there again: whereas saying mass first, the cunning dog fled for it a while, and came back again when the danger was over.

Notwithstanding these wise reflections, they remained in as much perplexity as they were the first day: they meet night and morning, they debate, they make processions three days and three nights; they oblige the *papas* to fast; you might see them running from house to house, holy-water brush in hand, sprinkling it all about, and washing the doors with it; nay they poured it into the mouth of the poor *vrykolakas*.

We so often repeated it to the magistrates of the town, that in Christendom we should keep the strictest watch at night upon such an occasion, to observe what was done; that at last they caught a few vagabonds, who undoubtedly had a hand in these disorders: but either they were not the chief ringleaders, or else they were released too soon. For two days afterwards, to make themselves amends for the Lent they had kept in prison, they fell foul again upon the wine-tubs of those who were such fools as to leave their houses empty in the night: so that the people were forced to betake themselves again to their prayers.

One day, as they were hard at this work, after having stuck I know not how many naked swords over the grave of this corpse, which they took up three or four times a day, for any man's whim; an Albanian that happened to be at Mykonos, took upon himself to say with a voice of authority, that it was to the last degree ridiculous to make use of the swords of Christians in a case like this. Can you not conceive, blind as you are, says he, that the handles of these swords being made like a cross hinders the devil from coming out of the body? Why do you not rather take the Turkish sabres? The advice of this learned man had no effect: the *vrykolakas* was incorrigible, and all the inhabitants were in a strange consternation; they knew not now what saint to call upon, when all of a sudden, with one voice, as if they had given each other the hint, they fell to bawling out all through the city, that it was intolerable to wait any longer; that the only way left, was to burn the *vrykolakas* entirely; that after so doing, let the devil lurk in it if he could; that it was better to have recourse to this extremity, than to have the island totally deserted: and indeed, whole families began to pack up, in order to retire to Syros or Tinos. The magistrates therefore ordered the *vrykolakas* to be carried to the point of the island, St. George, where they prepared a great pile with pitch and tar, for fear the wood, as dry as it was, should not burn fast enough of itself. What they had before left of this miserable carcass was thrown into this fire and consumed presently on the first of January 1701. We saw the flame as we returned from Delos: it might justly be called a "bonfire of joy," since no more complaints were heard against the *vrykolakas*; they said that the devil had now met with his match, and some ballads were made to turn him into ridicule.

All over the archipelago they are persuaded, that only the Greeks of the *Grecian* rite have their carcasses re-animated by the devil: the inhabitants of the island of Santorini are terribly afraid of these goblins. Those of Mykonos, after their visions were clearly dispersed, began to be equally apprehensive of the prosecutions of the Turks and those of the Bishop of Tinos. Not one *papas* would be at St. George where the body was burnt, for fear the Bishop should exact a sum of money of them, for taking up and burning a corpse without permission from him. As for the

Turks, it is certain that at their next visit they made the community of Mykonos pay dearly for their cruelty to this poor rogue, who became in every respect the abomination and horror of his countrymen. After such an instance of folly, can we refuse to own that the present Greeks are no great Grecians; and that there is nothing but ignorance and superstition among them?

www.ingramcontent.com/pod-product-compliance
Lightning Source LLC
Chambersburg PA
CBHW052013030426
42334CB00029BA/3208